CHILDREN'S COSTUMES

Other books in this series include:

Military Uniforms
Carol Harris and Mike Brown

Accessories
Carol Harris and Mike Brown

Women's Costumes
Carol Harris and Mike Brown

Men's Costumes
Carol Harris and Mike Brown

Festivals
Ellen Galford

North American Dress
Dr. Louise Aikman

Ceremonial Costumes
Lewis Lyons

Performing Arts
Alycen Mitchell

Everyday Dress
Chris McNab

Rescue Services
Carol Harris and Mike Brown

Religious Costumes
Ellen Galford

TWENTIETH-CENTURY DEVELOPMENTS IN FASHION AND COSTUME

CHILDREN'S COSTUMES

CAROL HARRIS AND MIKE BROWN

MASON CREST PUBLISHERS

www.masoncrest.com

Mason Crest Publishers Inc.
370 Reed Road
Broomall, PA 19008
(866) MCP-BOOK (toll free)
www.masoncrest.com

First printing 2002

1 2 3 4 5 6 7 8 9 10

Library of Congress Cataloging-in-Publication Data available

ISBN 1-59084-420-3

Printed and bound in Malaysia

Editorial and design by
Amber Books Ltd.
Bradley's Close
74–77 White Lion Street
London N1 9PF

Project Editor: Marie-Claire Muir
Designer: Zoe Mellors
Picture Research: Lisa Wren

Picture Credits:
Mike Brown: 5 (top right), 10, 23, 25, 28, 45. Corbis: 12, 29, 50, 52. The Culture Archive: 16, 18, 26, 30, 35. Kobal: 14, 39, 40, 47, 51, 53. Popperfoto: 5 (left), 6, 8, 9, 11, 20, 32, 33, 36, 43, 55, 56, 57. Topham: 5 (bottom right), 42, 48, 58.

Cover images: Mike Brown: main. The Culture Archive: bottom left. Popperfoto: background. Topham: top left.

Acknowledgment:
For authenticating this book, the Publishers would like to thank JONES NEW YORK.

Contents

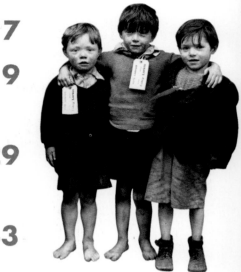

Introduction

Every day we go to our closets with the same question in mind: what shall I wear today? Clothing can convey status, wealth, occupation, religion, sexual orientation, and social, political, and moral values. The clothes we wear affect how we are perceived and also reflect what image we want to project.

Fashion has always been influenced by the events, people, and places that shape society. The 20th century was a period of radical change, encompassing two world wars, suffrage, a worldwide Depression, the invention of "talkies" and the rise of Hollywood, the birth of the teenager, the global spread of television, and, later, the World Wide Web, to name just a few important developments. Politically, economically, technologically, and socially, the world was changing at a fast and furious pace. Fashion, directly influenced by all these factors, changed with them, leaving each period with its fashion icon.

The 1920s saw the flapper reign supreme, with her short dress and cropped, boyish hair. The '30s and '40s brought a wartime mindset: women entered the workforce en masse and traded their silk stockings for nylon. During the conservative 1950s—typified by twin sets and capri pants—a young Elvis Presley took the world by storm. The '60s gave us PVC, miniskirts, and mods, and in 1967, the Summer of Love spawned a new language of fashion in which bell-bottoms and tie-dyed shirts became political expressions of peace and love. In the 1980s, power and affluence became the hallmarks of a new social group, the yuppies. Designer branding led the way, and the slogan "Nothing comes between me and my Calvins" started an era of status dressing. The 1990s will be best remembered for a new fashion word introduced by the underground street and music movement of Seattle, grunge.

Twentieth-Century Developments in Fashion and Culture is a 12-volume, illustrated series that looks at changing fashions throughout this eventful century, and encourages readers to question what the clothes they wear reveal about themselves and the world they live in.

Special introduction and consultation:
JONES NEW YORK

CHAPTER 1

1900–1940

The rapid expansion of communications over the last century has meant that the latest fashions—whether from New York or Paris—can be copied around the rest of the world within a few days. However, 100 years ago, fashions changed far more slowly.

Back at the turn of the 20th century, it took weeks, or even months, for new designs (usually from Paris) to reach the more isolated parts of midwest America, or even more remote areas of Europe. **Seamstresses** made patterns from drawings they copied of the latest fashions, usually from the new women's magazines. They were then able to make similar garments for those who could afford their services. Only the richest parents would buy ready-made or store-bought clothes for their children. For the most part, clothing was made

The lace collar (left) is typical of boys' formalwear at the turn of the century. The strapped shoes are unusual; boots were more common. The baby (right) could be a boy or girl—infants' clothes were often the same for both sexes.

by the local seamstress or by the mother herself, either by hand or on the recently invented sewing machine, although its use did not become widespread in the home until the 1920s.

A SLOW START

Of course, having the latest fashion was an indulgence limited to those who could afford it. For many parents at the turn of the century, the main concern was to see their children adequately clothed; whether this was in the latest style or not was hardly important. The slow spread of new fashions meant that children's clothes in the first 20 years of the century varied little from those of the previous 20 years, so wearing the clothes that your older brother or sister had grown out of was not such a big deal, as long as they were not too patched and stained. The same went for clothes bought secondhand or donated through the church or other charity.

Girls' fashions, like women's fashions, changed far more often and more radically than boys'. At the turn of the century, girls primarily wore knee-length, thick, cotton dresses with

A young girl is shown with her dog in 1918. Even after World War I, white cotton dresses with lace-trimmed collars and edges continued to be popular for formalwear; however, the hemline had risen quite sharply.

LITTLE LORD FAUNTLEROY

In the late 19th century, an American fashion in boys' clothes emerged that was widely adopted in Europe—which had traditionally set the fashions—and which had a long-lasting impact.

In 1886, Francis Hodgson Burnett, an English-born American, published *Little Lord Fauntleroy* and popularized the romantic style of the Cavalier or Van Dyck periods worn by the young American hero of the story. The look consisted of lace collars and ruffles; long, flowing hair; ribbons; and a velvet suit with knee-length pants, often topped off with a plumed or ribboned hat.

At the turn of the century, it was common for children to start working at an early age, and they generally wore handed-down adults' clothes rather than specialized children's clothing. Children dressed in **Fauntleroy suits** were obviously not employed in manual labor, and the velvet and lace used for the outfits were very expensive, so the suits became an instant statement of family wealth. The Fauntleroy suit, as it came to be known, was not particularly popular with the little boys forced to wear them, but struck a chord with a generation of proud American mothers, providing them with a means of displaying their economic wealth and a chance to imitate what they perceived as English aristoratic style.

The Fauntleroy suit was still worn, although not as commonly, up until World War I. Even today, it is sometimes worn by page boys at formal wedding ceremonies.

BUSTER BROWN

Today, Buster Brown is a name often associated with a successful American shoe company, but for many years, he was one of the best-known boys in 20th-century America, the hero of R.F. Outcault's popular comic strip of the same name. The strip first appeared in the Sunday comic pages of the New York *Herald* during the spring of 1902, and it continued to run until the 1920s.

Buster Brown was a mischevious child who, with his pet dog, Tige, and his sister Mary Jane, was constantly getting in trouble for playing pranks. His adoring mother dressed him in an immaculate tunic suit with a wide, white collar and large, floppy bow, and above-the-knee knickers. The outfit was so closely associated with the character that it became known as the "Buster Brown" suit. One of the first cartoon characters to be used for mass marketing, the marketing rights were licensed for a wide variety of other products.

long sleeves, round necks, and collars and cuffs of white cotton. Beneath this were long stockings and many undergarments. Hats and dresses were as frilly and detailed as possible. The relative wealth of a girl's family was shown by the decoration on the dress, which was usually in the form of **ruching** or **smocking**, or lace attached to the collar and cuffs. There was a belt at the waist, or a sash, usually in a dark color. Dark wool stockings were worn with ankle boots.

The other main form of girls' dress was the **pinafore dress**, a short-sleeved, white cotton **smock** worn over a darker blouse or dress. Girls' hats tended to follow the adult fashion, which was wide-brimmed and usually made of straw.

Formalwear for girls usually consisted of a dress of similar cut to normal everyday wear, but of better material—velvet or even silk—and if you could not afford that for the whole dress, then you could always have a silk or velvet sash. Alternatives included extra lace, or a dress all in white, often with matching white stockings. Like the Fauntleroy suit, it was completely impractical as children's playwear, but was ideal for formal occasions.

KNICKERS

Knickers—short for knickerbockers—were short, loose pants gathered at the knee. They evolved from knee breeches worn in the 18th century, but today they are generally associated with the 1920s and 1930s. Perhaps the greatest change in children's clothing in the early part of the 20th century was that little boys

---

MARY JANE

In 1904, John A. Bush, of the Brown Shoe Company, saw the value of the Buster Brown name as a children's shoe trademark, and the brand was launched at the St. Louis World Fair in the same year, and it remains one of the most famous brands of children's footwear in the United States today.

Mary Jane was Buster Brown's little sister, and as such, never received quite the same amount of attention. However, despite the fact that both children wore one-strap shoes (such as those worn by the little boy on page 8), the company decided to market this style as "Mary Janes." While the Buster Brown suit passed from fashion in the 1920s, "Mary Jane" is still used by Americans today to describe any shoe that sports the one-strap style—a style that is often worn by adult women, but which remains a classic for little girls the world over.

four and five years of age ceased to be dressed in skirts. These were replaced with romper suits or short pants, which first appeared about 1910. By the 1920s, children were dressing more casually and suits for young boys were increasingly taken out of the wardrobe only for formal occasions. Particularly for American boys, knickers and a simple shirt became more common as everyday attire.

Knickers came in a number of different styles—the main differences being the length and the degree of blousing. Boys old enough to go to school wore knickers with knee-length socks, and the first pair of long pants marked the transition from boyhood to manhood.

In the 1920s and 1930s, knickers also found their way into little girls' wardrobes as part of "knicker suits" (see page 18). This was in keeping with the penchant for androgynous styles favored by many adult women at the time, who had taken to wearing slacks and traditionally male clothing.

SCHOOL UNIFORMS

For most of history, children have worn scaled-down adult clothes, although from time to time, there have been periods of distinct children's fashions. Such a phase began in the latter half of the 19th century and owed much to a new educational system aimed at the middle classes—private schooling. School uniforms became increasingly common, and these were based on easily mass-produced styles.

This American boy wears a pair of knickers with long socks. These knickers are quite loose and reach below the knee. An English boy of the same age would probably have worn them a little shorter, at or just above the knee.

THE KNICKERBOCKER NINE (THE "KNICKS")

The term knickerbocker originated with the Dutch, who settled New York in the 1600s and wore pants rolled at the knee. The name Knickerbockers was first used in relation to a New York sports team when a baseball team from Manhattan named itself the Knickerbocker Nine. Early baseball teams not only wore knickerbockers, but also caps similar to those worn by English schoolboys. Modern baseball uniforms still use a variation of the knickerbocker. Aside from tradition, one practical reason for not wearing shorts when playing baseball is that having a leg covering helps to protect the skin when sliding into the bases.

For many children, their school uniform was their best outfit and was proudly worn to formal events. The boy's school uniform, as it existed for at least the first half of the 20th century in both the United States and Europe, was a product of English **Edwardian** fashions. The **blazer**, striped or with piped edges, was the latest thing for young Edwardian men in the summer, along with the closely fitting peaked cap. Worn with the school tie (usually striped) and shorts, this was the type of uniform worn by schoolboys in the 1950s.

THE ETON SUIT

One school had a greater influence on boys' fashions than any other. The famous English private school, **Eton**, spawned the **Eton suit**, the **Eton jacket**, the **Eton collar**, and even a haircut, the **Eton crop**. Eton, along with Harrow, were, and still are, the schools where the British aristocracy sent their sons, and many other schools in Britain, Europe, and the United States modeled themselves on them, including their somewhat distinctive uniforms. The Eton suit had a tight, waisted jacket with two long, vertical seams running down the front, worn with matching knee **breeches** and stockings, and an optional straw **boater** hat. Underneath was a white cotton shirt with a stiff Eton collar, a school tie, and an optional vest. All were worn with the inevitable leather ankle boots.

Modified Eton suits became very popular in the United States with young boys from affluent families—or at least with their mothers—and became the most stylish dress suit for two generations of American boys, five years old and up. They differed somewhat in style from the traditional British Eton suit: they were often worn with Peter Pan collars; the boater hat was replaced with a cap or no hat at all; and increasingly in the 1920s, the jackets had no lapels and the length of the knickers or pants varied. However, the name stuck, probably because it helped to generate appeal among American mothers who were used to looking to England for styles in men and boys' clothing.

THE SAILOR SUIT

Alternatives to the Eton suit included the Fauntleroy suit (see page 11) and the sailor suit. The main feature of the sailor suit was the naval-style collar. The suit could have short or long trousers, which could be normal width

These three variations of the popular sailor suit show different styles in pants, jackets, and hats. The naval collar is the distinguishing feature of the suit.

or **bell-bottomed**, and it came in a range of colors and materials, from canvas to velvet. The sailor suit, with its overtones of sea travel, pirates, and adventure, was a popular outfit among boys of the period.

For boys, the Eton suit and the sailor suit remained popular, even for formal Sunday wear, whereas the Fauntleroy suit was used only for the most formal occasions, such as weddings. Boys whose parents could afford cotton shirts wore an Eton collar. Their stiffness—achieved by a great deal of starching and ironing—made them limiting in terms of movement and, of course, uncomfortable. Boys were often told not to fiddle with their collars. Like adults' collars, they were separate from the shirt and secured by studs, which meant a great deal of fiddling and lost studs.

WORLD WAR I: SIMPLE, CASUAL, AND PRACTICAL

World War I (or the Great War, as it was then known) triggered a relaxation in manners and a simplification of dress for all age groups. Girls' styles reflected the concerns of adult women, for whom, during the hardship of war, detailed and overly tailored clothes were seen as a sign of privileged, selfish leisure. Patriotic women worked for the war effort and had no time for self-indulgent, showy clothes. Female munitions workers wore overall **frocks**, and dress designers, to give the impression of austere practicality, copied their plain styles. Following the lead set by children's clothes, skirts rose to calf length and were flared, which allowed greater movement, as did the new, soft, fullish **bodice** and more-flexible corset. For girls, too, the basic cut of their dress became loose, with no waist, or with a belt or sash loosely marking the hipline. The earlier trend for shortness continued, with girls' skirts now finishing just above the knee. Teenage girls wore their hair long, gathered with a bow at the nape of the neck and hanging from there either loose or in a braid.

Boys' clothes, too, became freer and far less restricting, especially in casualwear. Hand-knitting had become the "in" thing; pullovers rapidly

Dresses and Knicker Suits for Girls
Ages 7 to 14 Years

31L2800
Gingham
$1.59

31L2815
Organdie
$1.98

31L2830
Hills
Jean
$1.98

31L2820
Gingham
Bloomer
Dress
$1.00

31L2825
Separate Skirts
for Girls. Sizes 7 to 14

Big values in girls' nicely made plaited Skirts for wear with separate waists or blouses. Skirts are designed with button trimmed pockets and attached to sleeveless body lining. Your choice of five materials.
SIZES—7 to 14. State size. Shipping weight, 1¼ pounds.
31L2826—Cotton plaid...**89c**
31L2826—Navy blue Peggy cloth.................**89c**
31L2827—White jean......**98c**
31L2828—Khaki........**98c**
31L2829—Navy blue all wool serge.................**$1.98**

Crisp, cool **gingham** is combined with sheer **organdie** to make this little washable frock. Piping edges the short sleeves, organdie collar and loose hanging organdie panels on skirt.
SIZES—7 to 14. State size. Shipping weight, 1 pound.
31L2800—Lavender and white check.
31L2801—Blue and white check.
31L2802—Tan and brown check. **$1.59**

A Two-Piece Dress, made of reliable material. Separate blouse is of plain **Tokio crepe**. Collar and cuffs of white repp; attached belt; pearl buttons. The plaited skirt is of contrasting checked **gingham**, attached to a sleeveless body lining.
SIZES—7 to 14. State size. Shipping weight, 1 pound.
31L2805—Maize with black and white check.
31L2806—Blue with blue and white check. **$2.39**

Here are comfort garments, army style shirt, well made knickers and middy blouse. All are made of durable genuine Hill's Jean in Khaki tan. Don't confuse this splendid guaranteed fabric with ordinary cheap khaki—Hill's Jean wears like iron. Buy all three of these garments—they make a practical, easily laundered summer outfit.
SIZES—7 to 14. State size. Shipping weight, each, 1½ pounds.
31L2810—Khaki Knickers.
31L2811—Khaki Middy.
31L2812—Khaki Shirt. **98c**

Dainty Frock of sheer organdie, with panels of Swiss embroidered organdie bordered by insertions of fine Valenciennes lace. Trimming of Valenciennes lace edging. Back tucked in clusters and lace trimmed. Skirt is of embroidered organdie flouncing. Silk satin ribbon sash.
SIZES—7 to 14. State size. Shpg. wt., 1 lb.
31L2815—White. **$1.98**

Girls' solid comfort Bloomer Dress. Easily laundered and well made of fast color fancy **checked gingham**. Dress is trimmed with colored piping on the neck, sleeves, pockets, down front and around the bottom. Separate bloomers to match, with elastic at knees and waistband.
SIZES—7 to 14. State size. Shipping weight, 1¼ pounds.
31L2820—Red plaid.
31L2821—Blue plaid. **$1.00**

In this smart white Jean Two-Piece Middy Dress you'll find style and serviceability combined. The separate middy blouse has sailor collar and cuffs, trimmed with contrasting braid. Embroidered tie loop. Wide attached belt, fastening at sides with buttons. The plaited skirt is attached to a sleeveless body lining.
SIZES—7 to 14. State size. Shipping weight, 1 pound.
31L2830—White. **$1.98**

A Three-Piece Outfit to delight the active, healthy girl. Outfit includes comfortable knickerbockers; stylish sleeveless "meadowbrook" sports jacket, both made of finest quality iron wearing **Hill's tan khaki jean**; also a cool waist of washable white **cotton crepe**. Jacket has tuxedo revers, and belt of imitation leather. Knickers are in regulation style. These are well made "quality" garments.
SIZES—7 to 14. State size. Shipping weight, 2 pounds.
31L2835—Khaki tan. **$2.79**

31L2805
Crepe and
Gingham
$2.39

31L2810
Hills
Khaki Jean
Knickers
98¢

31L2811
Middy 98¢
31L2812 98¢

31L2835
Hills
Khaki
Jean
with Crepe
Blouse
3 Piece
Outfit
$2.79

A selection of post-WWI girls' clothes and hairstyles are shown in an American catalog. Note the low waistlines on the dresses, the sailor suit (top right), the knicker suits (bottom), and the bloomer suit (dress and bloomers, top center).

CROPPED CUTS

Hair, which had been worn long, was now cut far shorter for both women and girls, in a style often called the pageboy cut, ending at ear or chin length with straight bangs. This was sometimes unkindly called a pudding basin cut, from the earlier practice of cutting boys' hair by putting a pudding basin (dessert bowl) over their head and cutting off everything that extended beyond the rim, creating a practical, if somewhat severe, haircut. This shorter hairstyle was often hidden under a **cloche hat**, which pulled down over the head, causing the woman or girl to peer out from under the low brim, lending her a mysterious air.

Boys' hair remained resolutely "short, back, and sides"—and by short, they meant severely short—but quite long on top, usually with a side or even center part. Older boys especially greased their hair down, usually using **brilliantine** or **pomade**.

replaced the tightly buttoned vests of pre-war days, and knee-length knitted socks replaced the longer stockings.

FASHION BETWEEN THE WARS

By the 1920s, women's fashions had caught up with girls' clothes. Knee-length skirts were now the height of fashion, but they were worn straight, with the waist dropped to hip level, and girls' dresses followed this fashion. It was at this point that the gym slip began to appear, a sleeveless short dress with a square-cut neck, worn over a blouse or a knitted shirt. As its name suggests, it originally developed as an item of sportswear, but it was soon widely used as a school uniform. Ankle boots were now old-fashioned for girls, and shoes were pointed and strapped, as the fashion dictated. Like young **flappers**, girls began

American child star Shirely Temple made her film debut at the age of three during the 1930s. During the Depression years, her blond ringlets and dimpled smile, together with her song-and-dance acts, appealed to children and adults alike. Note the very high waist- and hemlines of her dress.

to wear sleeveless blouses, cloche hats, or a scarf tied around (short) hair—the Eton crop. Little girls, perhaps three or four years old, wore short skirts with large, matching **bloomers**.

By the 1930s, women's fashions had become far more figure-hugging, a style that was not suited to young girls, so once again, women's and girls' fashions diverged. Girls' dresses continued to be along the loose, flowing lines of the 1920s, although the waistline rose to the natural position, and the tops of their sleeves became puffed out or gathered. These changes led to the creation of a style that has lasted on and off ever since. Dresses were cut like a long shirt, buttoned right up the front. Known as the **shirtdress**, it came in heavy material with long sleeves for winter, and in light material with short sleeves for summer.

The main changes that occurred in boys' clothes up to 1940 were in the shape of the shorts and the shirt collar. The length of shorts slowly rose from a position just above the center of the knee to one about three to four inches (7.5–10 cm) higher by the 1930s. As the length rose, the width increased, from a tight fit to baggy. By the 1930s, the fashion for boys' formal clothing was to have an exact copy—long trousers and all—of their father's "monkey suit," as **evening suits** were commonly called then.

By the mid 1920s, stiff collars were no longer worn except at the most formal of schools, and were replaced by soft, fitted collars. In this, as in the length of women's skirts, children's fashions were leading the way; it would be at least 10 years before men could buy shirts with attached collars. Only those who were better-off wore cotton shirts. Far more common among poorer children were woolen shirts in a style known today as the polo shirt—or no shirt at all, but instead a round-necked sweater, homemade, of course. Meanwhile, hand-knitted sweaters remained popular among the better-off, especially in the patterned style known as Fair Isle.

By the 1930s, the sailor suit was still fashionable, but usually only for younger boys, although some girls' dresses from the period had sailor-suit necks. Toddler boys now wore "Buster Brown" suits, bright cotton shirts and matching shorts that were attached to each other with buttons (the shorts being extra large to go over the bulky diaper). For girls, the fashion was for matching coats and **leggings**, with the leggings going over the shoes, often secured by a strap under the instep.

Boys' jackets had changed, just as their fathers' jackets had. Schoolboys' uniforms were now far less restricting than the Eton suit. The style was now single- or double-breasted jacket, sometimes with a vest, worn with a shirt, either open-necked or with a tie. A few still wore knitted tops, sometimes with a shirt collar or polo neck. Boys' suits were scaled-down versions of their fathers' suits, but with short trousers. Like men's suits, they often came with a vest and a baggy, flat cap, both in the same material as the suit, usually serge, flannel, or tweed. Casual clothes consisted of short-sleeved shirts, pullovers, school blazers or sports jackets, and short or long trousers, depending on the age.

For both boys and girls, fashion as such remained almost entirely for those from better-off families. The poor continued to wear hand-me-down clothes or clothes their mothers had made. This was not so noticeable for boys—clothes that were 10 years old were virtually unchanged for them—but for girls, it was far more obvious.

UNISEX OVERCOATS

Boys and girls wore overcoats that were practically identical—in many cases, they could be buttoned up on either side, so girls or boys could wear the same coat. (Traditionally, women's clothes have buttons on the left side, while on men's clothes they are on the right.) Made of tweed, if possible, or wool, they were knee-length, waisted, and double- or single-breasted, sometimes with fur or velvet collars and cuffs (especially for girls). More-expensive girls' coats were waisted, cut to follow the general lines of the body. Another fashion for both sexes, up to the age of 11 or 12, was T-strap sandals with crepe soles.

INTERNATIONAL TRENDS

Internationally, there were a few differences between the dress of American and European children, but fashions were even then becoming broadly similar. French boys of the time tended to wear berets, while some German boys wore *lederhosen* (leather shorts) and peaked caps. In Britain, the Edwardian cap became almost universal for boys, whereas the fuller peaked cap was popular in the United States. Yet overall, there were similar sailor tops, shorts with knee socks, and jackets everywhere. Women's fashions, and therefore girls', were virtually the same everywhere.

SPORTSWEAR

In the 1920s, an interest in psychology brought about revised attitudes toward children and their development. Fresh air, sunshine, and exercise were suddenly considered very important to a child's well-being, and the introduction of

SWIMMING

When it came to swimming, poor children continued to do what children had always done, swim in the nude or in their **drawers**. The outfits of better-off children were scaled-down adult suits. At the beginning of the century, this meant long, two-piece cotton outfits for women.

The upper half was a long- or three-quarter-sleeved, thigh-length dress, while the lower half took the form of calf-length drawers. Girls' outfits also tended to be two-piece, made up of knee-length drawers with a matching or complementary top, similar to a sleeveless t-shirt. Boys wore a single-piece woolen suit that was similar to a combined undershirt and knee-length drawers.

Throughout the 1920s, the length of sleeves and legs shortened in line with dress styles, so that by the 1930s, swimsuits were substantially smaller. Both boys and girls wore an outfit similar to a woman's one-piece suit of today; the more daring people (or their toddlers) wore swim trunks.

sports and outdoor activities for children led to the development of less restrictive garments.

Bloomers were associated with Amelia Bloomer, a leader of the women's rights movement, who adopted the garment as everyday clothing to set an example to other women whom she wanted to free from the cumbersome, restrictive dress of the day. The original bloomers consisted of a close-sleeved jacket, a skirt falling slightly below the knee, and a pair of Turkish trousers gathered in above the ankles. The costume remained generally unpopular among women, but it did lead the way to more functional dress, particularly in sports. In the late 19th century, as more girls began pursuing education, many secondary schools adopted bloomer costumes for gym class and sportswear. Girls often wore middy blouses with their bloomers. These costumes were widely worn by girls through the 1930s. In the 1940s, schools adopted shorts for girls' gym uniforms, but a kind of bloomer-inspired romper suit was still worn by girls at some schools as late as the 1950s.

Today, there is often little distinction between sportswear and casualwear, but in the first half of the century, sportswear was strictly restricted to the sports field; it would be worn only for the event itself. In America, however, this tradition started to relax, often to the displeasure of more stuffy, conservative adults who still looked to Britain for leadership in fashion. In an article from *The Boys Outfitter* (1920), a commentator notes the difference in attitude between American boys and their English counterparts:

"Juvenile outfitting in this old country [England] differs fundamentally from what you find anywhere else in the world. The **shirt-waist** boy of America, for instance, is unknown. Boys take off jacket and waistcoat for games or a fight. But they do not go to...any scene of sport in the clothes which they will wear during the game. There is no necessity, we think here, to walk through the streets, or even along a country road, in what an English boy would consider only half a suit or even less."

American boys in the early 20th century played baseball more than any other sport, but there was little organization and few formal teams or uniforms. This began to change in 1930 when a clerk named Carl Stotz organized a three-team league, the beginnings of Little League.

At first, Little League grew slowly, due in part to World War II, which the United States entered in 1941. When American fathers returned from war in 1945, they often helped with their sons' teams. It became increasingly common for boys to have actual team uniforms, the first of which were bought at Kreseg's (now K-Mart). The standard baseball uniform was a cap, jersey, knee-length knicker pants, and long socks.

BOY SCOUTS

Founded in 1907 by Robert (later Lord) Baden-Powell when he held a camp for 20 boys at Brownsea Island, in England, the Boy Scouts proved an immediate success, with its emphasis on outdoor activities and earning proficiency badges. By 1910, the movement could boast a staggering 100,000 members. Scout organizations

This early Boy Scout wears long, narrow shorts and ankle boots. In many ways, this uniform did not change for nearly 60 years, except for his "lemon squeezer" hat, which was replaced by a beret in the 1950s.

On the cover of this 1920s British Scout handbook, the scout is wearing the official jersey top. The British Guides' book from the 1920s shows good examples of a leader's, Guide's and Brownie's uniform of that period.

sprang up in countries as far-flung as South Africa, India, Australia, Sierra Leone, Chile, and the United States, and a new section, the Sea Scouts, was formed.

The idea captivated youth from all over the world. In August 1920, just 13 years after the movement started with just 20 boys, the Scouts held their first "World Jamboree," and 8,000 boys from 34 different countries took part. Two years later, worldwide Scout membership had reached one million.

The first Scout uniform set a pattern that was to change very little in the years to come. At first, the boys wore a large, brimmed hat, turned up at one side, Australian-style. A flat-brimmed version soon replaced this style, which, due to the pinched crown, was often called a "lemon-squeezer." The rest included knee-length blue or **khaki** shorts; long socks "turned down below the knee with green tabbed garters showing on the outside"; a thick **bush shirt** in blue, khaki, green, or gray, with two breast-patch pockets and shoulder straps, or a jersey or sweater of the same color; and a neckerchief "worn loosely knotted at the throat and ends." The first Wolf

Cub uniform was a green cap with yellow piping, a green jersey, and a yellow neckerchief, worn with the normal long shorts and socks.

By the time of the 1929 World Jamboree, a large range of national variations was on show, many of which were in the form of headgear. Belgian Scouts wore berets, Norwegians and Brazilians wore side caps, and Poles wore peaked caps. More exotically, Indian Scouts wore turbans, while Algerians and Egyptians sported the fez. And there were some other styles: Scottish Scouts wore the kilt, of course, and Americans wore a jaunty plaid logger's jacket with the neckerchief worn over the top.

GIRL GUIDES AND BROWNIES

Baden-Powell had conceived the idea for boys of 11 years of age or older, but there were soon calls for girls and younger boys to be included. Gangs of younger boys invaded troop meetings, wanting to share the fun. At the first Boy Scout Rally in September 1909, the 11,000 boys who turned up for the march-past were followed by a rearguard of girls dressed in Scout jerseys, hats, and neckerchiefs, but with long skirts instead of shorts. Already 6,000 girls had registered as Boy Scouts by using only their initial instead of their first name. Giving way to the inevitable, Baden-Powell introduced a program for Girl Guides in December 1909, and by the following year, there were 8,000 Girl Guides in Britain.

In 1912, Juliette Gordon Low founded the Girl Scouts of America with just 18 girls. Four years later, a Brownies section was added. The Girl Scouts of America at first wore handmade outfits in blue **duck**, but these were soon replaced by ready-made khaki outfits, a long-sleeved, calf-length overall dress, worn with a leather belt, a troop tie, and a large-brimmed floppy hat, which by the 1930s, had a much smaller brim, like the cloche hats popular at the time. The name Brownies indicated the color of the uniform, a brown **overall dress** with a floppy hat, yellow tie, and knitted stockings.

CHAPTER 2

1940–1960

These two decades began with an austerity imposed by World War II, but they finished with fashion that suited the mood of the postwar world—more relaxed, more comfortable, more practical, and with a growing confidence in its sense of youth style.

"One front and one battle where everyone in the United States—every man, woman, and child—is in action. That front is right at home, in our daily lives." (U.S. President Franklin Roosevelt, in his address to the nation, in April 1942.) The 1940s were the war years, when shortages and "make do and mend" were the order of the day. Thousands

This American World War II poster urges children to make their contribution to the war effort. Note the simplicity of the clothes and the girl's knee-length skirt. Right, the First Lady Eleanor Roosevelt visits some Scouts in the kitchen as they prepare a luncheon to be held in her honor (April 1940).

SCOUTS, GUIDES, AND BROWNIES JOIN THE WAR

With the advent of World War II, the Boy Scouts of America (pictured below) now wore military-style caps, with a long-sleeved bush shirt, matching long trousers, and a neckerchief. By 1940, the Girl Scouts of America had been split into two age categories—the Juniors and Seniors—both of which wore berets. As with women's fashions, the dress, which in other ways had not changed, now had a higher, knee-length hemline.

In Britain, Scouts, Guides, and Cubs became very involved in war work. They acted as messengers for Civil Defence, learned first aid, worked in hospitals, and acted as "casualties" for first-aid classes and Civil Defence exercises. A total of 194 British scouts were killed in air raids while on duty.

of aircraft, tanks, cannons, ships, and so forth had to be built, so vast amounts of raw materials, such as steel, rubber, oil, fuel, and wood, were needed. Scarcest of all was manpower: men and women were needed for the forces and the armaments factories and other industries. Saving energy and materials was vital, and salvage (what we call recycling today) was fundamental. It was a patriotic duty to consume as little as possible and to recycle and repair wherever feasible.

RATIONING CLOTHES

Closer to where the war was actually being fought, the European situation was even more dire. Most of Europe was under Nazi control, and there, as in Britain, food and clothes were rationed. That meant that people were strictly limited in the amounts they could buy, even if they had the money.

In Britain, for instance, where clothes rationing was introduced in June, 1941, these were the suggested clothes that a teenage girl might buy with one year's ration coupons: one pair of shoes, six pairs of stockings, 10 ounces (285 g) of wool or 2 yards (1.8 m) of material to make into clothes, one suit, one overcoat, two slips, and one blouse. Or, she could buy one pair of shoes, six pairs of stockings, eight ounces (225 g) of wool or two yards (1.8 m) of material, one silk dress, two or three pairs of **camiknickers** or undershirt and knickers, two or three sets of **corselette** or brassiere and girdle, and six handkerchiefs.

For a teenage boy, this might be the year's ration: one pair of boots or shoes, six pairs of socks, one suit (no vest), one overcoat, collars, ties, or handkerchiefs. Or, he could buy one pair of boots or shoes, six pairs of socks, one pair of corduroy trousers, three shirts (silk or cotton), two pairs of underpants, two undershirts, and one pair of gloves. This might sound like a lot, but you might be amazed at how many clothes you go through in one year.

Children not only wore out their clothes, but grew out of them as well, so children's clothing exchanges were set up in Britain by the Women's Institute or by a group called the Women's Voluntary Services. Here, using stocks of clothes donated by American civilians, people took their children's outgrown clothes that were still in reasonable condition and exchanged them for larger clothes. These places also provided clothes for people whose homes had been bombed and who had lost all their possessions.

To make the most of their existing clothes, people were encouraged to follow the wartime slogan and "make do and mend"—this meant patching and mending existing clothes, or altering old clothes to make new ones. Demonstrations were given to encourage this, and there were exhibitions to show how clothes had been made this way. Newspapers and magazines printed patterns, and women's groups did much to encourage this practical attitude. A favorite thing was to undo old knitted items and remake them; make-do-and-mend books from the time show patterns not only for sweaters, scarves, and hats, but also for knitted underwear and swimwear. The underwear was often extremely itchy, while knitted swimsuits became incredibly stretchy and baggy when wet.

To save material, men's suits became single-breasted and trousers less baggy, while women's dresses became straighter and shorter. As usual, boys' and girls' clothes followed

A group of Dublin boys in 1948 wear poorly fitting hand-me-downs.

HITLER YOUTH AND THE BDM

In 1923, the Nazis in Germany set up their own youth groups based on the Scout movement. Their equivalent of the Boy Scouts, the **HJ** (*Hitlerjugend*) or Hitler Youth, wore a brown military shirt, black shorts (often *lederhosen*, the typical Alpine leather or suede shorts), long socks, a dark blue or gray ski cap, and a leather belt and buckle, from which hung the special HJ dagger. In cold weather, a **blouson** tunic was worn over the top; on this, or on the shirt, was worn the special HJ armband, bearing a swastika in a white diamond instead of the usual circle. The Hitler Youth acted as runners for the military, manned antiaircraft sites, and, by the end of the war, formed combat units, many of which fought with fanatical zeal.

The female equivalent of the Hitler Youth was the **BDM** (*Bund Deutscher Mädchen*), the German Girls League, whose activities were far less martial, reflecting the Nazi view that women should train to be good mothers and housewives. They concentrated on healthy activities, such as gymnastics, cooking, nursing, and "social work." The BDM had its own junior branch, the **JM**, the Young Girls.

suit. With this level of serious clothing shortages, schools could not insist that children wear the correct uniform, so children wore whatever their parents could manage to acquire.

Victory in Europe (VE) Day was celebrated in the United States and in Europe with parties and parades. Often, children wore homemade fancy clothes as part of the celebrations. However, the end of the war did not immediately mean the end of shortages. Most of Europe lay shattered, and children wore whatever they or their parents could get their hands on. In Britain, clothes rationing continued until 1949.

WOMEN WEAR THE PANTS

Trousers, a piece of clothing worn almost entirely by men before the war, were now worn by more and more women, and teenage girls started wearing slacks. These, of course, were the outfit of the factory worker, and thus gave the wearer the air of one doing her patriotic duty. Other wartime accessories, especially in heavily bombed Britain, included the tin helmet (children's versions were also available) and gas-mask bags or metal cases.

TEENAGE TRENDS

The war had put on hold the newly emerging teenage fashions. Most still went from children's fashions to adult clothes. At about the age of 14 or 15, teenage boys started wearing smaller versions of men's suits, which were sold with the option of long or short trousers. Teenage girls wore smaller versions of their mother's dresses, and stockings took over from socks. The new teenage look for girls was either girlishly feminine or boyishly casual. Their hairstyles started with long, loose hair, pinned up at the front and fastened with a band, or hanging loose from a side parting, perhaps even falling over one eye, in the wavy "peek-a-boo" style made fashionable by movie actress Veronica Lake. Blouses were popular in **gingham** checks with ***broderie anglaise*** trimming,

KIDS' HALLOWEEN COSTUMES

During the 1920s and 1930s, Halloween was regarded as an event for grown-ups. But from 1941 through 1945, while the United States was engaged in World War II, its adult citizens had more frightening things to think about than witches and ghosts. When peace returned, nest-building became a top priority. The result was a social phenomenon that began in the late 1940s and lasted until the beginning of the 1960s: the baby boom. As the numbers of children expanded, Halloween eventually became equated almost entirely with the young.

The toy industry quickly realized that there were vast profits to be made from the sale of colorful Halloween disguises. A handful of specialist costume manufacturers came to dominate the market, defining the styles seen on Halloween doorsteps for the rest of the century. Some of their wares reflected familiar Halloween traditions—kits containing all the necessary garments, masks, and accessories for the well-dressed witch, ghoul, or goblin. Others were the classic outfits worn for costume parties or school plays all year round: animal outfits, old-fashioned military uniforms, fur-trimmed royal robes and crowns, or apparel associated with classic storybook characters, such as Little Red Riding Hood.

35

Ninteen Fifties' schoolboys from Eton College are playing the famous wall game. They are wearing an interesting mixture of cricket sweaters, dark rugby shirts, and striped football shirts. One boy (right) is wearing the striped Eton school cap.

puffed sleeves, and wide, elasticized necklines that could be pulled down onto the shoulders. Alternatively, girls wore a tight sweater, either on its own or over a blouse whose collar went over the sweater. Skirts were of gingham check or woolen tartan, flared or gathered into wide waistbands. The outfit was finished off with white ankle socks and wedge-heeled sandals.

The boyish, or "tomboy," look was made up of long hair taken back into a knot or tied into two side bunches. A long, baggy sweater known as a **sloppy joe** came next, worn with a straight skirt, slacks, or blue jeans with the legs rolled up to calf length, and the obligatory white ankle socks and gym shoes. Sloppy joes and baggy trousers or jeans were also the dress of fashionable teenage boys, who, together with their partners, would dance to the latest music—jive, boogie-woogie, or jitterbug—or talk among themselves in the fashionable slang, thus excluding and bewildering their parents.

POST-WORLD WAR II: AMERICA TAKES THE STAGE

During the 1930s, American culture, as dictated by Hollywood, began to have a great influence, especially on the young. Now, to a Europe devastated by war and suffering from crippling shortages, rationing, and hardships, the United States appeared to be a land whose streets were paved with gold. Anything American was, by its nature, good. Teenagers longed for the styles they pored over in American magazines. Boys, especially, followed American styles: casual t-shirts or brightly patterned or checked sports shirts, worn with military-style battle-dress tops, waisted and zipper-fronted. In a major departure from prewar styles, hats became unfashionable. Before the war, a man would have felt almost undressed without one, but now a hat was definitely for old men only. Hair was still short at the back and sides, but an increasing number of young men also wore it short on top, in the crew-cut style. Those who continued to wear it long on top let it hang more naturally, without the use of grease.

Europe—in particular, Paris—was still a mecca for fashionable women, and it was from Paris that Christian Dior launched his **New Look** in 1947. The full, figure-hugging lines of the New Look were not altogether suitable for girls with adolescent figures, but teenage girls were able to adopt it to some degree. Skirts and dresses were cut fuller, with gathers or flares, and long, calf-length hemlines. For everyday wear, the more casual American styles were popular, so skirts were either very full or very narrow, and blouses and sweaters had soft, natural shoulders, as opposed to the prewar puffed or padded shoulders. Calf-length slacks, which became known as **pedal pushers**, were also adopted from American fashion. All-black outfits were considered quite sophisticated and appeared on many young women as party outfits.

1950s & 1960s: THE BABY BOOMERS

For younger children, things changed much more slowly. In the 1950s, boys were often wearing exactly the same clothes as the boys had 15 years previously—although a growing minority could be seen in long trousers or jeans, usually with four- to six-inch (10- to 15-cm) cuffs. **Windbreakers**, usually woolen—either plain or plaid—with elastic at the wrists and bottom edge, had become popular during the war and continued to be so. Shirts were still made of thick material, although plaid was popular for both shirts and ties. For those who could get them, t-shirts were becoming trendy. Handknitted sweaters and **slipovers** were still common, especially among poorer children. Sneakers were common in the summer, as were Wellingtons in the winter, worn with overcoats or raincoats, a knitted **balaclava helmet**, or the ubiquitous school cap.

For girls, short floral cotton dresses remained fashionable, usually worn with short white socks and sandals, although a few lucky girls might be seen in slacks. In winter, a knee-length, double-breasted overcoat or raincoat provided protection from the weather, worn with Wellington boots. Kilts were popular, worn with knee- or ankle-length socks.

A whole range of typical children's clothes and hairstyles from the 1950s can be seen here. Notice the gingham dresses, the white ankle socks, shorts, T-shirts, and the absence of ties—small boys now only wore ties for special occasions.

The biggest change in children's clothes was in the use of new manmade fibers, such as polyester, acrylic, and nylon. Clothes made from these were less expensive, easier to wash and iron, and lasted much longer—every mother's dream.

BOBBY-SOXERS AND BIKERS

In the United States, the teenage girls wearing this new relaxed style, often with their hair tied up in a pony tail, were called **bobby-soxers**, named after the short bobby socks that completed their preppy look. Bobby-soxers had their own musical heartthrobs, chief of whom was a new singer, Frank Sinatra.

Teenage boys might choose to look like a member of the increasingly common motorcycle gangs by wearing a leather jacket, white t-shirt, and jeans. However, this look was associated with rebelliousness, and it was generally unpopular with parents. One episode of *Leave It to Beaver*—a popular TV sitcom that dealt with the everyday travails of being a young boy growing up in the 1950s—dealt with this theme. The young hero, Beaver, reminds his mother that he needs a new jacket and that he would like a leather one with an eagle on it. His mother responds: "Beaver...I know you need a new jacket but I have told you repeatedly and your father has told you that you may not have a leather jacket with an eagle on the back. We do not want our son looking like a roughneck."

As an alternative to this "roughneck" look, boys and adolescents might choose to wear a more stylish outfit of sports jacket (often plaid) with a usually open-necked shirt, sweater, and trousers that flared out from the waist.

As the world recovered from the war, a postwar boom began. Full employment became normal, and the 1950s became a time of increasing prosperity, which began to show itself in an explosion of youth culture in music, fashion, and films. This was the start of a completely new teenage movement, a time of rock 'n'

Hayley Mills, a teenage movie star of the 1950s, is dressed in a casual style, with pedal pushers— a particularly American look—and a softly draped blouse. Braids also became a popular style for girls in this period, and it remains so today.

SPORTSWEAR

For gym classes, both boys and girls wore baggy shorts—boys in undershirts, girls in t-shirts. Older girls wore short skirts or gym slips, usually with thick drawers underneath. Interestingly, up to this point, the length of skirts for activities such as tennis had roughly followed the fashion for daywear, but now, as the fashionable length for skirts dropped, the length for sports skirts continued to rise. Fashionable teenage girls wore tennis dresses that, like regular dresses, were more figure-hugging than before, with frilly petticoats. Ski suits were in far brighter colors and strong checks; ski pants were much tighter; and elasticized materials were increasingly used.

For swimming, boys were now universally in trunks, while girls wore a one-piece suit with a rubber swim cap. For older teenage girls, the two-piece, or bikini, as worn by French movie star Brigitte Bardot, was the latest thing if you had the figure, and the nerve, to wear it—and if your parents did not find out.

roll music played on jukeboxes and of "squares" and "hep cats" meeting at soda fountains.

European teenagers watched their American contemporaries on newsreels and in movies, such as *Rebel Without a Cause*, starring James Dean, and *The Wild One*, with Marlon Brando, and they longed to be part of the new "scene," meeting in coffee bars and copying the American clothes and talk. New singers, such as Bill Hayley and the Comets, Buddy Holly and the Crickets, and, of course, Elvis Presley, were condemned by parents and religious leaders as purveyors of "the devil's music." However, teenagers all over saved to buy the records of this latest music, made all the more attractive by their parents' disapproval of it. This new youth scene was something the older generations were not used to; they did not understand it and they did not like it.

CHAPTER 3

1960–1980

In this period, fashion for the young became more outrageous and more varied to reflect people's different attitudes and lifestyles, ranging from hippie and ethnic to hot pants and sneakers.

1960–1970

The 1960s, like the Roaring Twenties, would go down in history as a decade of great fun. Certainly, the prosperity of the 1950s continued, so most people could afford to be part of the fashion scene. However, the "Swinging Sixties," as they were dubbed, did not actually start in 1960, but a few years later. In the beginning, 1960s' fashions were not particularly daring; skirts were quite short,

A young Michael Jackson (1972) sports an Afro hairstyle, which was popular at the time. The highly patterned, brightly colored outfit is typical of 1970s' style. A 1960s' toddler (right) wears a brightly striped t-shirt and dungarees, clothes that reflect the bright, brash, fun feeling of the age.

above the knee, but no higher than they had been in the 1920s. The dominant hairstyle for women was the **beehive**, a high, full look achieved by back-combing and a lot of hairspray, which made the hair stiff and unmovable. One of the fashion icons in this period was the First Lady, Jacqueline Kennedy, who popularized a style of **pillbox hat** that became named for her.

By 1963, however, the style that was to become forever associated with the 1960s was beginning to emerge. The moves toward softer, more informal fashions that had gathered pace throughout the 1950s were beginning to gel into a definite look. A complete change of emphasis was taking place. Before the war, teenagers had tried to dress and look "grown up." Then, in the 1950s, they had adopted their own younger fashions—and now the grown-ups wanted to join in the fun. Fashions generally became younger, as adults tried to look younger, and the whole emphasis was on youth.

Slacks were worn by more and more women, but with a lower waist than ever before. **Hipsters**, as they became known, were worn with wide belts in contrasting colors. Jeans continued to grow in popularity, although the fashion

---

BEATLEMANIA

Youth culture was everywhere. In 1963, an English band from Liverpool had taken Britain by storm, and "Beatlemania" soon spread throughout Europe and the United States. The Beatles' particular look—collarless jackets, elastic-sided **Chelsea boots**, and haircuts that look short to us, but were almost outrageously long in 1963—were soon being copied by millions of young people, and clothing manufacturers gave them what they wanted. Boys grew their hair long in their own versions of the "mop top" style so detested by many of the older generation. Schools dusted off their dress codes, and many young men were sent home to get a "proper" haircut.

MINIS FOR MINORS

The mini, as the miniskirt soon became known, was alarmingly short, and at first few women or girls would dare to wear them, but they very quickly became widespread. However, many schools had banned them, and newspapers reported girls being sent home for wearing them to school. One schoolgirl of the time remembers an easy solution: "At school we used to turn our waistbands over to make our skirts really short." And, of course, if you came face to face with the principal, you could always simply roll the skirt back down to the longer length.

became ever tighter. In contrast, hipsters flared out from the knee down in bell-bottom style, only slightly at first, but widening slowly as the decade went on.

Following the Beatles' huge success, everything British became fashionable, and the center of the fashion world moved from Paris to London. In the mid-1960s, British designer Mary Quant introduced pantyhose and the miniskirt, both of which had a great influence on women, and even girls. Pantyhose were a particular boon. Now, girls could abandon the socks that had always singled them out as different from their older sisters (stockings, and the garter belts that went with them, were not always suitable for schoolwear). Pantyhose, on the other hand, were ideally suitable, and almost overnight, long socks and ankle socks disappeared from teenage fashions. The perfect complement to the miniskirt was long boots, either just below the knee or thigh-length. "**Kinky**

THE DENIM REVOLUTION

Blue jeans had been worn by boys and teenagers since the 1950s, but in the 1970s, denim really came into its own, with denim shoes, jeans, dungarees, skirts, dresses, long and short jackets, vests, and hats—worn by both sexes, formal or frayed, tailored or patched.

On toddlers, children, teenagers, and adults, denim was everywhere. It was ironic, yet perhaps inevitable, that a fabric originally used for workmen's clothes, which had become the uniform of antiestablishment types, became so universal that it turned into the very establishment it was supposed to show rebellion against. It was this that led to its decline in the next generation.

boots," as they were known, came in a variety of materials—leather, suede, or preferably wet-look plastic—and a vast range of colors.

While minis were seen as scandalous on older teenagers or women, on younger girls, short skirts looked perfectly natural, and the bright, floral prints they came in also added to the effect. And that was just the look that the designers were trying to achieve. This was a great time to be young. Everything was about youth: the music, the arts, and the fashions.

For younger girls, a stylish yet practical style emerged. Short shift dresses, worn over ribbed sweaters (often polo-necked) and with matching ribbed tights, made an outfit similar to their mothers'. Both girls and boys wore slacks, dungarees, and jerkin-type tops in an extension of the **unisex** style introduced into adult fashion.

By the late 1960s, the styles were once again changing. In San Francisco particularly, the "Flower Power," or hippie, movement was blossoming, a reaction against such realities as the Vietnam War, pollution, and rampant consumerism. Long hair, either flowing or tightly permed into a gigantic "Afro" cut, was worn with flowing ethnic-style clothes, preferably handmade.

In an early example of sports gear used for everyday clothes, the **anorak**, previously an item of ski wear, caught on as an all-purpose winter jacket, and has remained so ever since. Like other items of ski wear, the anorak had benefited from the use of modern fibers to become light yet genuinely water- and windproof, while modern design had seen it evolve from drab tones to bright reds and blues, and even combinations of several colors. It had thus become a perfect blend of the functional and the stylish, a path that many other items of sportswear would also take.

1970–1980

By the early 1970s, there was an overabundance of fashion styles, which created little more than confusion. The focus of fashion shifted from Paris to London, and then to San Francisco,

The cast from the popular television show *The Brady Bunch* are wearing outfits that are typical of the 1970s, including Cindy's (far left) short dress.

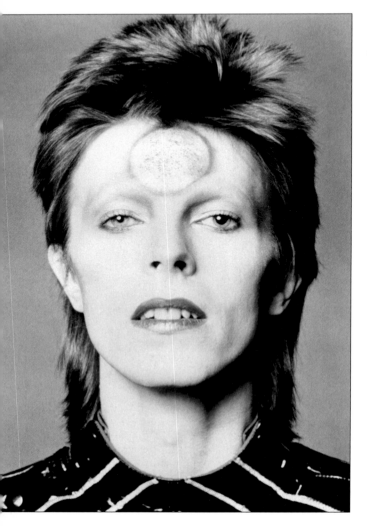

David Bowie was a glam rock icon of the 1970s. With his feathered hair, makeup, and outrageous clothes, Bowie was a symbol of teenage rebellion. His makeup became even more extreme and colorful as the decade wore on. He was also largely responsible for the spread of the "shag" hairstyle, which beame incredibly popular during the 1980s.

where it seemed to dwindle and fade, leaving no definite direction to follow. As a result, little in the way of new fashion emerged in the first part of the decade. One exception was the successor to the mini: **hot pants** were tight, very short shorts, often in satin—and a fashion that looked best on younger women and teenagers.

Hair stayed long, but became far more styled, using layering and feathering. Children, too, were treated to the new hair designs. They also shared in the latest footwear fashion, the **platform sole**, either on shoes or boots. This extremely built-up style suited short people—and that included children, as far as shoe designers were concerned—far more than tall people, on whom it looked a bit silly.

Children benefited from a rapidly expanding market. As the teen market had developed in the 1950s, so now the children's fashion market was the growth area, paid for by the still-booming economy and, more directly, by parents who had themselves been teenagers in the 1950s and 1960s and for whom children's fashions seemed a good thing. The hugely popular anorak-

SNEAKERS

The most successful fashion crossover from the sports industry was, in many ways, the strangest of all. Sports shoes, which were known as sneakers, became the most sought-after fashion item. Prices for some styles were astronomical, and newspaper stories abounded of children mugged for their sneakers. Once again, fashion had turned the world on its head: 20 years before, sneakers or gym shoes were worn by poor children or those from orphanages or reform schools.

type jacket—along with the leather (or leather-look) and sheepskin-style flying jacket—almost killed off the traditional children's overcoat.

Parents and children alike enjoyed brightly colored, flared corduroy pants, jeans, and dungarees. Worn with t-shirts, **cheesecloth** shirts, or denim shirts, and blouson-style zippered jackets or denim jackets, these made a comfortable, practical, yet fashionable outfit, pleasing both children and their parents.

Outrage was the watchword of the 1970s' most remarkable fashion development, the punks. Starting in urban Britain as a reaction to the cozy fashions and music that had begun to take over in the mid-1970s, punk was designed to alienate and offend. Based around leather, zippers, outrageous t-shirts, luridly colored Mohican-style hair, and multiple body piercings, punk was a movement almost entirely for teenagers.

T-SHIRTS TAKE OVER

Punks were not the only ones to wear t-shirts, of course. Previously, t-shirts were used, often for children, as a simple slip-over top. In the 1950s, they came in white; in the 1960s, they were a canvas for tie-dyeing; and in the 1970s, they became carriers for designs, slogans, artwork, and embroidery.

CHAPTER 4

1980–2000

Early in the 20th century, children wore smaller versions of adult fashions. As children's clothes became more practical, they led the way in styles. By the end of the century, the revolution was complete: for leisure time especially, adults started to dress like children.

Reversing the tradition of dressing children as small adults, adults began to wear fashions that had first become popular with children—specifically, teenagers. Long shorts and baggy sweatshirts, sneakers, and t-shirts marked a triumph of practicality and comfort over style. Mixtures of synthetic and natural

A teenager (left) wears a loose shirt and long, baggy shorts. This style among skateboarders became a trend for boys—and men—in the 1990s. Drew Barrymore (right), a child star of the 1980s, wears a sweater over a shirt.

fibers, such as polyester with cotton, were common. Such clothes could be washed at low temperatures, dried quickly, and did not need ironing.

STAR GAZING

At the same time, when children and teenagers dressed up, they were more likely than ever to wear fashions dictated by designer labels and pop stars. The pop star Madonna was a major influence on girls' fashions. Her style combined imagery from her Catholic background, such as crucifixes and rosaries, with revealing clothes, especially underwear worn as outerwear. **Basques**, spaghetti straps, and cropped tops that showed the midriff became commonplace.

Glam rock had popularized makeup in the 1970s as something that teenage boys, as well as girls, could wear. This went one stage further in the early 1980s with teenage fashion movements, such as the New Romantics and the Goths, who drew inspiration from old horror films and 18th-century poets, pirates, and highwaymen. The

Teenage girls of the 1980s were able to copy Madonna's early look simply by wearing rosary beads around their necks and tying strips of colored material or lace in their hair. Note the lacy, fingerless gloves.

KUNG FU KIDS

In the 1970s, David Carradine starred in the TV series *Kung Fu*, about a Chinese Buddhist priest in the Wild West. It was a great success and opened the way for a spate of martial arts films from Bruce Lee, as well as *The Karate Kid* movies of the 1980s and the *Teenage Mutant Ninja Turtles* television series and movie in the 1990s. Some children's fashions sprang from this: karate headbands, Chinese slip-on sandals, and kimono-style pajamas, to name a few.

For younger kids the Turtles were everywhere. Leonardo, Donatello, Michelangelo, and Raphael, were to be found on pajamas, t-shirts, hats, socks, and underwear. Kids could pretend to be their favorite Turtle, aided by the bandanna masks, belts and other accessories available in all the toy stores.

influences of gay liberation meant that a person's gender was less defined by what one wore. The British singer Boy George, of the band Culture Club, wore makeup and dreadlocks in a manner that could be imitated by both male and female fans, in a new slant on the unisex fashions of the 1960s. For a time, during the 1990s especially, the craze with both sexes for earrings—in one ear, both ears, or multiple earrings in each—was supplemented by the craze for piercing any part of the body and for tattoos.

GRUNGE

Like the hippies of the 1960s and punks of the 1970s, the grunge style of the 1990s was a youthful reaction against the crass and empty commercialism of the fashion and music industries. It was a style and approach eagerly seized on and exploited by those same industries. Typically, loose-fitting and often ragged sweaters were worn with savagely torn jeans. Grunge fashions were originally derived from charity and thrift shops, but you could pay a small fortune for versions and variations that had designer labels and came from outlets that were more expensive. Camouflage trousers and tops were initially part of a revival in Army surplus clothing. Soon, the patterns of camouflage were used on everything from handbags to t-shirts.

The icon of grunge was Kurt Cobain, who led the group Nirvana; when he committed suicide, the grunge movement lost its momentum. Cobain's suicide was linked to a family history of mental illness and to his heroin addiction, the latter typified by an undernourished and abnormally pale look. The grunge look had horrified many members of the older generation, who failed to understand that this was exactly the desired effect of this rebellious teenage fashion. Supermodels of the time, such as Jodie Kidd and Kate Moss, summed up this look on the catwalks, emphasizing pale faces and a body that looked emaciated. The controversy these images caused and the concerns of adults, especially parents, did little more than make the fashion appealing to would-be rebellious teens. It was soon out of fashion among them, however, simply because it was "last year's style."

SPORTS

The Olympic Games increasingly set fashion trends in casual clothing, for children as well as adults, and other events, such as the 1994 soccer World Cup, held in the United States, encouraged children to wear the shirts and shorts of their national or local teams.

DESIGNER KIDS

Designers who made their names with adult fashions, such as Dolce & Gabbana (D&G) were now also promoting ranges of clothing for children. Chain stores, especially Gap, producing low-key, casual clothing for adults found they could sell much the same garments to children of all ages. Labels and logos, especially on sneakers, t-shirts, and other items from the sportswear industry, developed their own appeal for children and teenagers.

Meanwhile, the baseball cap—which might be said to have started the trend for sportswear as fashion for children—was now seen the world over, with logos for every imaginable product, worn by people of all ages, and with almost every type of outfit. It is amazing that a piece of sports clothing from a game almost entirely confined to North America should have become almost global in its use. The baseball cap has found its way into the uniforms of schools, the armed forces, and such groups as the Wolf Cubs in countries where the sport is virtually never played.

LYCRA

Another crossover from the sportswear industry was Lycra. With its stretchy, clinging qualities, Lycra was an exciting yet practical fabric for both designers and those who wanted to imitate sporting icons of the time. Elsewhere in the world, replica soccer

A group of young bat boys for the Montreal Expos watch as a batter makes it back to home base. These boys are wearing protective helmets, but one of them (center) also wears a standard baseball cap underneath. The style of the pants is reminiscent of knicker pants worn in the 1930s and 1940s (see pages 13–15).

This 1999 designer boyswear would not have looked out of place on a boy of the 1940s: the blouson jacket and the hand-knitted sweater were both popular at that time. It is an excellent example of how fashion often repeats itself.

outfits were in great demand, creating a boom industry, with designs changing every season to match those worn by the pro-fessional soccer teams. In the United States, the sporting heroes of the 1980s were such athletes as Carl Lewis and Florence Griffith-Joyner, the latter instantly iden-tified by her spectacularly long, decorated fingernails and one-piece running suits.

SCOUTS, GUIDES, AND BROWNIES

The efforts made in the previous decade to prevent the move away from organized youth groups continued, and the rapid drop in membership was halted. The movement to modernize dress also continued. In 1984, the Daisy Girl Scouts were introduced for five-year-olds. Their basic uniform was a blue tunic top, to which can now be added blue shorts and tights and a blue and yellow baseball cap. The Brownie uniform consisted of a dark brown skirt, a blue shirt, long socks, and a sash worn diagonally over one shoulder. This forms the basic uniform for Junior and Cadette Girl Scouts as well, except that for Juniors, the skirt, socks, and sash are in green with a white shirt, and for Cadettes, khaki with a white shirt. Seniors have a sleeveless windbreaker instead of a sash.

OVERVIEW

The 20th century saw children's clothes changing for practical reasons, durability, and comfort, while new, cheaper materials and growing prosperity meant that an ever-increasing number of families could afford such fashions. In this way, children's fashions began to set trends, both in the use of new materials and in the creation of more comfortable, casual styles and patterns. By the end of the century, the cult of youth meant that children's styles were setting the trend for adult fashions, with sports clothes becoming ever more commonly worn.

This young girl is carrying a Pooh Bear backpack on her back. The backpack became a fashion accessory in the 1980s, and children's novelty versions, like the one shown here, soon appeared. Like many children's fashions, "novelty" backpacks crossed the boundary into adult fashion for a while.

DIAPERS

For the first half of the century, babies were almost entirely wearing the traditional diaper made up of a square or rectangle of linen, cotton flannel, or stockinet, folded once diagonally to form a triangle, the two long arms of which were brought around the baby's waist, while the shorter arm was passed between the baby's legs. All three corners were then brought together in front and fastened with a safety pin, or better still, a diaper-pin. The absorbent cloth might be covered with a tightly knit wool "soaker" to improve containment.

Washing and drying these diapers, which had to be changed several times a day, kept mothers busy. There were attempts to create disposable diapers, but they were not successful. Rubber pants that went over the diaper were introduced in the 1940s. These kept the diaper from leaking and allowed mothers to take their babies out more. In the 1950s, they were replaced by plastic versions.

In the 1960s, came the first really practical disposable diapers. These were a godsend for mothers—gone were the piles of smelly washing and the lines of drying diapers! Over the next few decades, diapers went through inevitable improvements in the way they were fastened, in absorption, dryness, and so on. Another innovation was to have bright designs printed on them.

Recently, with more people becoming concerned about the environment, there has been a movement away from disposable diapers, which every year create thousands of tons of waste, as well as using up vast stocks of raw materials. Now, terry-toweling diapers are no longer just white, but are produced in a whole range of brightly printed designs, including teddy bears, whales, and frogs, which means babies and toddlers can be dry and fashionable. Meanwhile, for the makers of disposables, the focus has been on producing a fully biodegradable, eco-friendly diaper.

GLOSSARY

Anorak originally, a ski jacket

Balaclava helmet a knitted hat covering the entire head, like a ski mask

Basque a tight-fitting bodice worn by women

BDM German girls' youth movement for 14- to 21-year-olds

Beehive a 1960s' high, full hairstyle for women

Bell-bottoms trousers that flare, or "bell," at the bottom

Blazer colored, often striped, summer jacket, or school uniform jacket

Bloomers early 20th-century name for women's undershorts; named after American Amelia Bloomer

Blouson a short, blouse-shaped jacket

Boater flat-topped straw hat with a brim

Bobby-soxers American teenage girls, named after their short socks, in the 1950s

Bodice the part of a dress above the waist

Breeches short trousers, fastened below the knee

Brilliantine an oily hair dressing

Broderie anglaise open embroidery on white linen or cambric

Bush shirt a type of thick shirt with shoulder straps and breast pockets

Camiknickers combined undershirt and underpants for women

Cheesecloth very rough cotton fabric

Chelsea boots 1960s' elastic-sided boots worn by men

Cloche hat 1920s' woman's hat that pulled down over the ears

Corselette combined brassiere and girdle

Drawers undershorts

Duck strong, untwilled cotton used for sails or sailors' clothing

Edwardian the first decade of the 20th century, named after Britain's king, Edward VII

Eton a famous English "public" (that is, private) school

Eton collar a broad, stiff collar usually worn outside the jacket, named after Eton School

Eton crop a short, cropped hairstyle, long on top, named after Eton School

Eton jacket a short jacket named after Eton School

Eton suit a boy's suit with an Eton jacket and shorts, named after Eton School

Evening suit a man's formal suit with a tuxedo jacket

Flappers young fashionable 1920s' women

Frock a dress

Gingham plain cotton cloth in a check pattern

Girl Guides European Girl Scouts

HJ the Hitler Youth, a Nazi organization for 14- to 18-year-old boys

Hipsters 1960s' trousers with a hip-level waist

Hot pants very short shorts for girls (1970s)

JM junior branch of the Nazi girls' movement for 10- to 14-year olds

khaki brown-green color used for military and Scout uniforms

kinky boots 1960s' long boots for girls

Lederhosen leather shorts, as worn in the Alpine regions of Eastern Europe

Leggings close-fitting stretch pants

Little Lord Fauntleroy a character from a book of the same name, whose name implied vanity about one's clothing

New Look feminine look launched by Dior immediately after World War II

Overall dress a loose dress worn over other clothes

Pedal pushers 1940s–1950s calf-length slacks worn by women and girls

Pillbox hat small, round hat

Pinafore dress a collarless, sleeveless dress worn over a blouse or sweater

Platform sole 1970s' built-up sole on a shoe

Pomade scented hair dressing

Ruching a frill or gathering of lace

Seamstress a woman who makes clothes for a living

Shirtdress a dress cut like a long shirt, buttoning up at the front

Shirt waist a woman's tailored garment, usually a blouse or dress, with details copied from men's shirts

Slipover a light, usually short-sleeved sweater

Sloppy joe a long, baggy sweater

Smock a loose, shirt-like top, with the upper part gathered in smocking

Smocking an ornamental effect made by gathering material tightly into pleats, often with stitches in a honeycomb pattern

Unisex a style of clothing or haircut designed for both men and women

Windbreaker a short, windproof jacket

TIMELINE

1870 School uniforms are used in middle- and upper-class schools.

1907 Robert Baden-Powell founds the Boy Scouts in Britain.

1909 Baden-Powell introduces a program for Girl Guides.

1912 Juliette Gordon Low founds the Girl Scouts of America.

1914–1918 World War I (the Great War); fashions become simpler and more practical.

1917 United States enters World War I.

1914 Wolf Cubs founded.

1916 Brownies founded.

1920–1930 The Roaring Twenties: short dresses, cropped cuts, and cloche hats.

1920 First World Jamboree, in which 8,000 Scouts from 34 countries take part.

1930–1940 The first teenage fashions appear, although only for the rich.

1933 The Hitler Youth becomes the official German youth movement; the Boy Scouts and other youth groups are banned in Germany.

1939 World War II begins in Europe.

1941 U.S. enters World War II; clothes rationing introduced in Britain.

1945 End of World War II.

1947 Fashion designer Christian Dior launches his "New Look."

1949 Clothes rationing ends in Britain.

1950–1960 Beginning of mass teenage fashions, starting in the U.S.

1960s Disposable diapers available in stores.

1965 Mary Quant introduces the miniskirt.

1967 The Summer of Love: the height of the hippie age.

1975 Punk style is born.

1980s Madonna becomes a major influence on girls' fashions; rap music and fashion hits the streets.

Early 1990s Grunge music and fashion emerge from Seattle.

FURTHER INFORMATION

BOOKS

Brown, M. *A Child's War.* London: Sutton's Publishers, 2000.

Buck, Anne. *Clothes and the Child: A Handbook of Children's Dress in England 1500–1900.* Carlton: Ruth Bean, 1996.

Harris, Carol. *Collecting Fashion and Accessories.* London: Octopus, 2000.

O'Brien, Joan. *Children's Folk Costumes.* New York: Dover Publications, 2002.

Tierney, Tom. *American Family of the 1930s.* New York: Dover Publications, 1988.

ONLINE SOURCES

The Costume Gallery

www.costumegallery.com/children.html

This site is mainly for costume designers, but it has some interesting and useful sections regarding children's clothes.

Historical Boys Clothing

http://histclo.hispeed.com/index2.html

A comprehensive Web site with an astounding amount of information about all aspects of boy's clothing, with sites for presidential boys' clothing, royalty, and youth uniforms. As well as general commentary, exerpts are provided from relevant literature, cinema, and TV shows, as well as personal accounts of different eras and their fashions from men who experienced them.

Scout Web Sites

www.girlscouts.org; www.scouting.org

History, uniforms, and artifacts of the Boy and Girl Scouts of America.

Studio Bambini **Magazine**

www.studiomagazines.com/studiobambini/ main.html

Online home to *Studio Bambini*—a magazine filled with the latest international designer clothes for toddlers to pre-teens.

ABOUT THE AUTHORS

Mike Brown lives in London, England, where he writes and teaches part-time, in addition to giving talks and lectures on 20th-century history and architecture. He has written several books about everyday life during World War II: *Put That Light Out* (Sutton, 1999), *A Child's War* (Sutton, 2000), and, with his wife, Carol Harris, *The Wartime House* (Sutton, 2000).

Carol Harris is a freelance journalist specializing in the 1920s, '30s, and '40s. She has contributed to exhibitions at the Imperial War Museum on wartime fashions and utility clothing, and regularly gives talks on these and related topics. Other books include *Collecting Twentieth-Century Fashion and Accessories* (Mitchell Beazley 1999), and *Women at War—in Uniform* (Sutton, 2002).

INDEX